# MOTIVATING READERS

# MOTIVATING READERS

*Teaching in the Post Pandemic Era*

CAROLYN WAHL

Carolyn Wahl

# Copyright

Copyright © 2023 by Carolyn Wahl

All rights reserved. This book or any portion thereof may not be reproduced or used in any manner whatsoever without the express written permission of the author except for the use of brief quotations in a book review.

Printed in the United States of America

First Printing 2023

ISBN 978-1-961214-01-9

For information and permission to quote this book in any length or form contact the author via www.middleschoolcafe.com

# A Note from the Author

Thank you for picking up this book and allowing me to be part of your educational journey. Before you begin the book, I want to take some time to express my appreciation for you as a teacher. Teaching is not an easy job and each year it seems to get a little more challenging.

While we are not in the profession for the awards or the accolades, it is nice to hear that you are appreciated and you are doing a good job. It might be cliche to say that you were the reason someone smiled today, but it is true!

A mentor once told me that even on the hardest days, on the days when students tested my patience the most and made me question my life choices, I still made a difference to a child in my class. I think of that sentiment often when things get challenging in class.

It is so easy to get bogged down with all the negativity surrounding education - believe me I know there's a lot, but don't lose sight of all the amazing things that happen because you chose to be a teacher.

I want to start this book off by appreciating you and all you have done and are doing to support the needs of your students.

To you, I say **THANK YOU!!!**

## *Changing Landscape of Education*

The COVID-19 pandemic had a profound impact on every aspect of our lives, and education was no exception. In March 2020, teachers were asked to essentially reinvent education overnight. We had two weeks to revamp how we teach. We had to learn how to conduct classes over

Zoom, how to connect with students through a computer screen, and we had to figure out multiple online programs in an attempt to keep students learning until the end of the school year.

The transition was not easy for anyone. Just as teachers struggled to shift, students struggled to adapt to the new online format. I believe most students did the best they could under the circumstances. Did they always show up to class? No. Did they always participate? No. But we don't know their life circumstances. We don't know what happened while they were at home. Some students did not have access to the internet or were required to share a computer with multiple family members and could not attend classes even when they wanted to. Without the in person connection with the teacher, many students simply tuned out. Consequently, their education was severely disjointed.

When we returned to the classroom, it quickly became evident that pandemic online education only widened the learning gaps that already existed. Students returned to classrooms with higher behavior concerns and lower skill abilities despite the best efforts of teachers. Teachers are struggling to bridge the gaps created by the pandemic.

I find myself struggling to meet the high needs of my students. Their skill levels vary greatly and it's challenging to adapt to each of their needs effectively, especially when the gaps are so wide. Sometimes, I even question my own abilities to teach and wonder if teaching is still the right path for me.

I know I'm not alone in this struggle. Teachers are burning themselves out trying to meet the much higher demands of students, administration, and society. Is it any wonder why teachers are leaving the profession in such large numbers?

So as you read this book, and as you have conversations with your colleagues, your curriculum mentors, your administration, and your district representatives, I want to encourage you to shift the conversation. Students aren't behind - yes, there are learning gaps, but no, they're not behind; they are exactly where they should be given the circumstances they have had to face. That doesn't mean there's no hope. There is hope, but we have to start looking at it differently.

## A Mindset Shift

It is important to acknowledge that disruptions in education are not unprecedented. Over the years, natural disasters like floods, hurricanes, and fires have caused students to miss school for extended periods of time. However, we did not write off those students or their teachers, instead, we provided them with the support they needed to help them succeed. Those students went on to graduate, and become doctors, lawyers, and other productive members of society.

Many districts, administration, and politicians are acting like school continued as normal during the pandemic - it didn't. They create expectations and policies that assume the students who came back to our classrooms have the same abilities as the students before the pandemic and that's simply not true. Any teacher can tell them that! In my opinion, districts and politicians must stop fixating on the idea that students are behind and instead focus on ways they can support students with their current needs.

It's easy to get caught up in this mindset, thinking our students are behind. They are only behind when you compare student abilities with the skill levels of students pre-pandemic. That is an unfair comparison. With the world shut down and classes online, the resources and support available to students during the pandemic, compared to what was available pre-pandemic, were severely lacking. The circumstances were vastly different and therefore, the outcome was different.

Returning to the classroom after the COVID lockdown has been a difficult adjustment. It's almost like going through a grieving process because so much has changed since March 2020. Our entire world was turned upside down and we're just now beginning to recover. However, I know that change starts with me. That's why I wrote this book - to inspire and empower teachers to do what's best for their students. Block out the noise of the world and do what you do best - meeting the needs of your students!

I want teachers to know they don't have to change everything they know about teaching, but they do need to make some adjustments to accommodate the new normal of student abilities. We can still use old lesson plans, activities, and teaching methods, but we need to tweak them to suit the current needs in the classroom. For instance, we may need to teach skills that previously were a given, such as teaching students how to write a topic sentence when they used to come to our class knowing how to write an entire paragraph.

As we continue to recover from the effects of the pandemic, we need to accept where students are currently, rather than pushing to catch them up. It's important we stop trying to teach the standards from two years ago plus the standards from today because that simply isn't going to work. Instead, we need to focus on closing, or at least shrinking, the learning gaps. This is a much different conversation and process than simply trying to catch them up.

To close these gaps, we need to change our mindset as teachers and pull forward areas that we can. For example, if we're teaching a lesson on figurative language but our students don't yet have the vocabulary for it, we need to pause, teach the vocabulary, and then continue with the unit. We can't change the current unit to simply define and identify figurative language, which may be a lower grade level standard. We need to keep moving our students forward, but we also need to fill in the gaps in their knowledge. Even if we haven't had to teach certain concepts before, as secondary teachers, we need to be willing to adapt and teach what our students need to succeed.

As teachers, students, administration, and even society attempt to recover from the long term effects of the COVID pandemic, we need to stop pushing to *catch* students up and accept where students are now. I am optimistic that with proper support, students will recover from pandemic losses, improve their skills and be able to graduate just as students impacted by natural disasters have done in the past. It is up to us as professionals to do what we know is right for our students, despite what others want to tell us. We are the only ones that can change what happens in our classrooms.

## The Why Behind the Book

I wrote this book because I wanted to provide teachers with strategies and insights to inspire them in the midst of an ever changing educational system. As a teacher still in the classroom, I understand the challenges that come with teaching during this unique time. This book provides teachers with principles, techniques, and insights to help navigate these uncertain times. It outlines strategies for bridging gaps in student knowledge, adapting teaching methods to accommodate different learning needs, and providing meaningful instruction. I hope this book will give teachers the confidence they need to continue making a positive impact in the lives of their students.

Many good teachers have already left or are considering leaving the profession due to these seemingly impossible challenges surrounding education right now, but I strongly believe there is hope. Hope that we can reach each student and help instill a love of learning. Hope that we can help each student move toward closing their own learning gaps. Hope that we will come out of this pandemic in a better place than when it began.

Even though things are different, all is not lost. We can still inspire students to love reading. We can connect students with books that allow them to dream. We can help students see the world differently through the written word. We don't have to change everything that we've ever done. We just have to learn to adapt what we know how to do in order to meet the needs of today's students.

Many of the ideas you'll read in this book are not new. I didn't create them. I didn't invent them. But what I hope to have done for you is show you how you can use your secondary ELA teaching strategies in a new way. Outline how you can loop back to what students may have missed, fill in those gaps, then move them along their education journey.

Ultimately, I wrote this book because I believe that education can still be successful in spite of the challenges and obstacles we have been presented with. With the right support and strategies, teachers are capable of helping their students become successful learners and making a real difference both in and outside their classrooms.

# Contents

*A Note from the Author*   vii

1. A Shift in Education   1
2. Create a Culture of Reading   9
3. Reigniting the Spark   26
4. Motivation through Goal Setting   46
5. Using Technology to Enhance Learning   56
6. Navigating the New Educational Landscape   69

*Meet the Author*   75

# I

# A Shift in Education

*If a child can't learn the way we teach, maybe we should teach the way they learn.* -Ignacio Estrada

The COVID-19 lockdown of 2020 had a profound impact on education. The sudden shift to remote learning and the disruptions caused by the pandemic resulted in significant gaps in students' education. As teachers return to the classroom, they are faced with unprecedented challenges of addressing these gaps while also dealing with the trauma and anxiety that many students experienced during the pandemic.

The students who returned to the classroom after the lockdowns are not the same as the ones who left. Many have lost critical instructional time, missed out on social interactions, and faced challenging circumstances. Students came back to the classroom with gaps in their education that are larger than ever before, resulting in disengaged and apathetic students.

The pandemic has brought significant changes to the way reading is taught and learned in the classroom. Many students are struggling with focus and motivation, affecting their ability to engage with reading materials. Mental health challenges such as stress, anxiety, and depression have made learning harder for students and have contributed to a decrease in their interest in reading.

This book aims to provide teachers with strategies to help their students become more confident and engaged readers despite the challenges of the pandemic. We will explore the impact the pandemic has had on English Language Arts (ELA) education and provide practical solutions to address the gaps in student learning. The goal is to equip teachers with the tools they need to create effective literacy instruction that meets the unique needs of today's student.

## *Education During Lockdown*

During the 2020 lockdown, teachers had to quickly pivot and essentially reinvent school overnight. Teachers were faced with the daunting task of adapting to online instruction and learning new online programs and teaching methodologies with little to no training.

Just as teachers were struggling to teach online, students were struggling to learn online. And for multiple reasons, many students did not, or could not, jump on board. Some did engage in online learning activities but it simply wasn't the same. It was harder for teachers to reach all students, everything took longer online than it would have had they been in the classroom and the gaps (when compared to grade level standards) widened. When students returned to the classroom, skill levels were in a deficit, student reading levels were lower than ever before and student willingness to participate in learning had greatly diminished.

To address these challenges, it is essential to acknowledge the impact of the pandemic on education and take a more strategic approach to teaching. Rather than pushing students to catch up with pre-pandemic standards, educators need to slow down and assess the unique needs of each student. This includes addressing the gaps in knowledge and skill development that emerged during the pandemic and identifying strategies for supporting students in their learning.

One key factor in making this shift is to recognize that not all students are necessarily *behind* due to the pandemic. While some students may have fallen behind, most simply have gaps in their learning. A learning gap is a lack of a foundational skill causing a disparity between what a student can do and what is expected at a particular grade level. A student with a learning gap may be able to demonstrate proficiency in some areas at grade level while they fall short in others. This makes sense when we think of how students were able to participate in school, especially at the height of the pandemic.

By changing the conversation, from *students are behind* to *students have gaps in their learning* we can see a greater need to differentiate instruction. We have to acknowledge that the skill level of students as a whole has changed. Instead of being frustrated and upset, we need to figure out the new normal so we can meet students where they are and focus less on where we think they should be.

Ultimately, the key to overcoming the challenges the pandemic brought is to adopt a student-centered approach to learning. By prioritizing the unique needs of each student and creating a supportive, engaging learning environment, teachers can help students overcome their learning gaps and emerge as confident learners. With the right support and strategies, we can ensure every student has the opportunity to succeed despite the challenges they have faced.

### *Rethinking the Approach*

Teachers have always had a full plate, but in this new era of education, we find more being pilled on. Students, and subsequently the teachers, now have to deal with decreased abilities and increased levels of stress, anxiety, and depression which makes learning feel nearly impossible. Many students have lost interest in reading and their ability to focus has shifted which makes learning a constant struggle. Teachers must strive to foster an environment that promotes resilience and lifelong reading habits in students if they hope to fill in the learning gaps created by the pandemic. To maximize student engagement, teachers need to be creative and flexible with their approaches to literacy instruction.

If teachers are going to reengage students in reading, they have to change their focus in literacy instruction. Prepandemic secondary ELA had a large focus on the love of literature - the shared experiences through characters in books. Classroom discussions could revolve around relating to the characters, conflict, and events of the plot. However, in the post pandemic era, that focus has to shift to include developing basic reading skills. It is becoming more and more common for students to come to class with skill deficits, and secondary teachers are finding themselves teaching basic reading skills which they may not feel equipped to address.

During the lockdown, many students missed important foundational skills whether that was due to extended school closures or lack of participation, it really doesn't matter. Students may not have the skills necessary to meet grade level standards they are expected to know now that we've returned to the classroom. It might not be that students are unwilling to do what is asked, it might be that they truly don't know how to do it.

In this new era of education, teachers need to be open to teaching ideas and concepts they previously did not need to teach in order for students to meet the grade level standards. Skills across the board took a hit during the pandemic and it will take time to recover what was missed.

Rather than throwing out everything you know about teaching, teachers should focus on making adjustments to lessons to better meet the needs of students today. This can include incorporating technology, using real-world examples to make lessons more relatable, or providing opportunities for students to collaborate and work together. All things teachers were already focused on prior to the pandemic.

We have to get past the thinking that students two, four, six, or more years ago could do so much more and read higher level books. Because you know what? You're right! But one thing to remember is the students sitting in our classrooms today have been through a worldwide shutdown - a time when every adult in their life was facing the unknown. This created a sense of uncertainty for students and their education suffered despite the valiant efforts of educators. So rather than focus on the idea of what has been or what could have been under different circumstances, we need to focus on what we can do *now* and how we can help the students *now*.

As teachers navigate the post-pandemic era, they should recognize that traditional teaching strategies can still be effective, but they need to rethink how they deliver their lessons. While some strategies may need adjustment to meet the needs of students, teachers don't have to change everything they know about teaching. Instead, teachers should be flexible and creative in their approach to literacy instruction, including more differentiated options and student choices to tailor teaching methods to meet the needs of their students today. Teachers need to focus on adapting and refining their existing teaching strategies, which will most likely include teaching skills that were traditionally below grade level.

Teaching skills below grade level can help students fill in the gaps and build a stronger foundation for future learning. When students have a strong foundation of basic literacy skills, they are better equipped to tackle more complex concepts and texts, and are more likely to feel confident in their ability to read and comprehend.

Additionally, teaching skills below grade level can help boost student motivation. When students feel like they are making progress and seeing success in their learning, they are more likely to feel motivated and be engaged. By providing targeted instruction and support to help students build foundational literacy skills, teachers can help students feel confident in their ability to read and learn.

By meeting students where they are and providing the support and instruction they need to fill in gaps in their knowledge, teachers can help students to become successful readers and lifelong learners.

## *Student-Centered Approach to Teaching*

Developing a more student-centered approach to teaching involves focusing on the individual needs, interests, and learning styles of each student. This is more important now than ever before. With the learning gaps being so wide and varied, the more teachers can adapt and adjust lessons to meet individual needs, the more engaged students will be.

Differentiation is a key factor in creating a truly student centered classroom. Differentiation is not a new concept but prepandemic it was mostly associated with meeting the needs of special education students or addressing the needs of high achievers.

Differentiation involves tailoring instruction and assessment to meet the ability levels of individual students. This may involve using a variety of teaching strategies, providing students with different learning resources, or modifying assignments and assessments to accommodate for the gaps in student learning.

While it is not reasonable to expect a teacher to create 30 or more individual assignments for students, a teacher in today's academic climate must be willing to provide students with options for learning and demonstrating proficiency in an obtainable way for the student. Utilizing strategies and teaching methods that have built-in options for differentiation is going to increase the teacher's ability to reach more students.

It may also be time to rethink the use of whole group instruction. With short attention spans and a wide array of learning gaps, small group instruction may be a better option. Traditionally small group instruction was seen mainly in the elementary classroom, but with the increased need to target specific skills to fill in gaps, small group instruction is something secondary teachers need to consider.

A student-centered approach to teaching is vital in today's academic climate. It requires teachers to be flexible and adaptable in meeting the needs of individual students. Differentiation through a variety of teaching strategies and resources is key to creating a learning environment conducive to today's students. By implementing more student centered strategies, teachers can ensure that each student is receiving the support they need.

## *Adapting to the New Era*

Teachers are facing unique challenges in improving student reading levels in the post pandemic era. It's important to recognize that students are not collectively behind in their reading skills after experiencing two years of disrupted learning - that would be a much easier problem to solve! Rather, students have varied learning gaps and are at different levels of readiness to return to *life as usual*. Therefore, it's essential for teachers to adjust strategies to meet the needs of their students.

One effective strategy is to provide students with choice in the books they read, also known as choice reading, a method centered around differentiation. This method can be accomplished by utilizing the school and classroom libraries or including digital reading materials. Another strategy is to use small group instruction or station work to differentiate instruction and meet the needs of individual learners, especially struggling readers. With the wide range of abilities in each classroom, these activities allow teachers to easily differentiate to reach more students and move them further along their educational journey.

Book talks, where students share their thoughts and opinions about books they have read, can also be an effective way to promote reading engagement. When students hear their peers talk about books they enjoyed, it can motivate them to read more and explore new genres and authors. This can help create a culture of reading in the classroom and encourage students to view reading as an enjoyable and valuable activity.

Peer discussions help students explore different perspectives and develop a deeper understanding of the text. Through these discussions, students learn from each other, build on each other's ideas, and broaden their own perspectives.

Fostering a collaborative learning environment through book talks and peer discussions can help students to develop their critical thinking and communication skills, which are essential for improving reading comprehension and overall motivation. Students learn to analyze and interpret texts, make connections to their own experiences and the world around them, and are better able to articulate their thoughts and opinions in a clear and concise manner.

Today's students are digital natives who have grown up surrounded by technology. Incorporating technology into literacy instruction is another way to keep students engaged and motivated to read. Students are accustomed to accessing information through digital devices and are often more comfortable with technology than with traditional learning methods. Therefore, incorporating technology and multimedia resources into literacy instruction can be an effective way to reach more students.

Technology also provides opportunities for personalized learning. Students have access to materials when they need them. For example, students can access digital libraries, e-books, and audiobooks, which can provide a wide range of reading materials at their fingertips. Interactive activities such as online quizzes, games, and simulations can also help to keep students engaged and motivated to read. This approach can be particularly helpful for students who are more visually oriented in their learning.

It's crucial for teachers to approach post-pandemic literacy instruction with a growth mindset and recognize that each student has their own unique learning journey. Teachers must recognize the unique challenges students face and adapt their strategies to meet the needs of all students. By implementing effective strategies such providing choice, fostering collaboration, and utilizing technology, teachers can create a learning environment that is engaging and motivating, ultimately leading to improved reading comprehension and overall improved literacy levels. In the following chapters, we will explore how teachers can use these strategies to better motivate their students to read.

# 2

# Create a Culture of Reading

*Reading should not be presented to children as a chore or a duty, it should be offered to them as a precious gift.* -Kate DiCamillo

Creating a culture of reading means creating a classroom that places a value on reading. Anyone who spends time with your class would be able to see a classroom filled with students engaged in reading and discussions about books, literature, and life. Creating a culture of reading in your class means having a classroom where student voices are respected and students are encouraged to make choices in their reading materials. Encouraging students to read on a regular basis will help them develop strong reading skills and develop a lifelong love of reading.

By cultivating an environment conducive to reading in the classroom, teachers can help students grow – not only developing strong reading skills but also discovering the joys of literature! In this chapter we will explore different ways to create a classroom culture that encourages a love of reading with your students: from writing book reviews to holding meaningful discussions about books, there's so much that you as their teacher can do to encourage a lifelong love of learning through literature!

Remember that reading is not just about academic achievement, it also has the power to develop empathy, expand worldviews, and foster critical thinking skills. By promoting a love of reading in your classroom, you are helping to prepare your students for a lifetime of learning and growth.

## *A Teacher that Reads Leads Students to Read*

As the teacher, you set the tone for reading in your classroom. By being an active reader, you not only help contextualize and deepen discussions about reading with your class; but you also send an enthusiastic message to students, encouraging them to develop their love of books!

It is important to stay up-to-date on the latest books your students may be interested in. No, you don't have to read every book, but having an awareness of what's available can go a long way in motivating and inspiring students. If you know the current releases and trends, you can make more relevant suggestions and recommendations to your students.

Firsthand experiences with books of various genres and styles provide teachers the opportunity to share their experiences and spark curiosity. Excitement for reading is contagious - so don't be afraid to share what you're reading!

## *Student Choice*

**Give students more ownership over their reading choices.**

At its core, student ownership of learning is about the transfer of knowledge and skills - the ability to take what they have learned and apply it on their own. When it comes to reading, ownership means empowering students to utilize skills with the confidence needed to become lifelong readers. When teachers give students ownership over their reading choices and let them select books that interest them, they unlock the keys to motivation and unleash the power of reading. When students have a say in what they read, their enthusiasm for reading grows and engagement increases.

Students that select books based on personal interest are more likely to stay engaged in the book because it resonates with them. When students enjoy something, they naturally commit to doing it for longer periods of time. When students can choose their reading materials, they are more invested in the story and they seek out time to read on their own. They read because they want to know more about the characters or to see what happens next in the story. By allowing students to have ownership over their reading choices, they are more likely to read which will build the skills necessary to become lifelong readers. You may even find your students talking about what they are reading outside of the classroom!

Part of student choice is giving students permission to abandon a book they don't like or just isn't a good fit. If a student begins a book and gets 30-40 pages in and they really don't like it, it doesn't do anyone any good for them to struggle through the next 200 pages. There are many books to choose from - have them return the book and pick up a new one.

Reading should be a pleasurable and engaging experience, and forcing a student to read a book that is not enjoyable can lead to frustration and a negative attitude towards reading.

Abandoning a book that is not engaging or meaningful can free up time and mental space for students to explore other books they may find more interesting and enjoyable. It can also encourage them to be more selective and discerning in their reading choices, which can help them develop a stronger sense of their own reading preferences and tastes.

Reading is not a one-size-fits-all activity, and what works for one student may not work for another. By allowing students to abandon books that don't resonate with them, teachers can create a more inclusive and empowering reading environment that values the diverse needs and interests of all students.

Encouraging students to abandon books that they don't like can help them develop a positive attitude towards reading and promote a culture of choice and empowerment in the classroom.

**Peer-to-Peer Recommendations**

Teachers often share books they think their students will love, and often they do, but there is something to be said for peer recommendations. Students are more likely to accept a book recommendation from a trusted friend than their teacher.

**Book Reviews**

Encourage your students to make their mark on the classroom library shelves by writing book reviews! Not only will this help students engage with books they're unfamiliar with, but it will also create a chance for others in the class to explore and connect over something enjoyable - reading!

There are many low prep ways to engage students in book reviews:

- Have each student leave a review on a sticky note and then place the sticky note on the inside cover of the book for others to discover.
- Create a student review section in your library – just like you would find at any bookstore's "staff recommends" area.
- There are many premade forms for book reviews but you don't have to be fancy either. Don't be afraid to use a simple note card or half sheet of paper and tape it to the bookshelf or hang on a bulletin board.

Students should share why they like the book and what type of reader might enjoy it. If the book is part of a series, they should include that information as well.

Creating a rating system can also be a fun way to engage students in evaluating and discussing books. This can be done in a variety of ways, such as assigning a numerical score or using a visual representation like stars or emojis. Get students involved in the creation of the rating system and encourage them to explain their ratings. This can help students develop a deeper understanding of what makes a book enjoyable or not.

Writing book reviews encourages students to think critically about what they've read while communicating their opinions to others. This is an excellent way to promote the books that students love and foster meaningful conversations about literature. Allowing students to have a dedicated space for their reviews gives them a sense of pride and excitement thus increasing their motivation.

## Book Trailers

Creating book trailers or "book commercials" is also a great way to engage students with book recommendations. Book trailers allow students to be creative and incorporate technology to promote the books they are passionate about. Challenge students to create inspiring book trailers that capture readers' attention and encourage others to pick up a new favorite story.

Creating book trailers can be a fun cooperative learning activity perfect for a culminating activity after a book club unit is completed. By working in groups, students can share ideas, collaborate on production tasks, and provide feedback to one another. This not only promotes teamwork and collaboration but also provides an opportunity for students to learn from one another and develop interpersonal skills.

By providing students with the opportunities to share their favorite books, teachers can inspire a deeper love of reading while promoting critical thinking and creativity. These activities offer an excellent opportunity for students to showcase their reading accomplishments!

## *Access to Books*

### A classroom library that represents your student population

Having a classroom library filled with books that students can access at any time provides an inviting and accessible space for students to explore their interests. Allowing students to view the library and make suggestions of must-read titles helps foster excitement, engagement, and ownership when it comes to independent reading.

Fill your classroom library with books your students want to read. Too often teachers focus on having a high volume of books and don't pay enough attention to the quality of books. Make sure your shelves are stocked with books that represent the diversity of your student and community population. When students see diverse characters, backgrounds, and perspectives they can relate to, they are more likely to find the books interesting to read.

By having books your students relate to, you can create an atmosphere of respect and inclusion that will help your students explore the world through reading. As a result, you will have students that are engaged in reading and excited to choose their next book.

A diverse library also allows students to develop a better understanding of different cultures, religions, and lifestyles. Furthermore, it encourages inclusion and respect for diversity within the classroom by celebrating the similarities and differences among people.

Diverse books also lead to meaningful conversations about topics such as racism and inequality that may not otherwise be discussed. By introducing these topics through age-appropriate books, students learn to appreciate and accept each other. Ultimately, having diverse books in the classroom is a great way to foster a more inclusive learning environment where everyone feels appreciated and valued.

But how do you find these books? Begin by checking your local library for a selection of currently recommended books, which can provide insights into what students in your area are reading. Another valuable resource is visiting nearby bookstores, as they can offer a glimpse into the interests of students within your community. Additionally, don't hesitate to consult other teachers within your school or district about the books their students are engaging with. By tapping into the reading preferences of students nearby, you increase the likelihood of finding captivating books that will resonate with your own students.

Also, don't be afraid to ask students what they like. They may not be able to suggest a title, but they can suggest topics that interest them so you have a place to start.

Throughout the year pay attention to what your students are reading. Are there specific topics or authors they gravitate towards? Do they prefer books in verse or graphic novels? Add those types of books to your library. It is more important to have books in your classroom library your students will read than to have a beautiful collection of books no one will pick up.

A word of caution, if you are checking out suggested book lists, remember they are curated for the masses. You may find some great suggestions, but if they are not books your students will read, they won't help you motivate your students.

Be sure to review your bookshelves each year and don't be afraid to get rid of books your students are not reading. By doing this, you can ensure your library is up-to-date with books that are motivating and will encourage students to read. Take inventory of the materials in your library and decide if there is anything that needs to be removed, replaced, or added. Taking time each year to review your classroom library can go a long way in helping you ensure students are getting the best classroom library experience.

Students love to help with this. In the last few weeks before the end of the year, ask a few responsible students - students who you also consider readers - to pull titles they think should be removed. Have them set the books aside for you to look at so you can have the final word on whether they stay or go. You'll be surprised at how accurate they are most of the time. If a book has been on the shelf since the retired teacher left it behind three years ago and no one has touched it, here's your permission to remove it!

**Schedule Regular Library days**

Teachers should take their students to the school library, as it nurtures an appreciation for books and informational resources. Going to the library gives students access to a wide range of books and resources. Libraries encourage students to be independent thinkers and regularly visiting the school library can foster a love of reading and an appreciation for learning that will stay with them long after they leave school. If teachers do not take students to visit the school library, some students may never get to go or even see the value in it.

How excited are your students about school library days? In elementary school, students go to the school library weekly or at least a couple times per month, but in middle and high school, the amount of dedicated time for visiting the library dwindles to almost nothing. Some teachers never take their students to the school library.

Building excitement for going to the library begins in the weeks and days before the actual library visit. Begin by posting the date of the library visit to create a sense of excitement and anticipation. As the day gets closer, mention it more often in your conversations with students or as part of your daily 'get your class started' routine. Build the day up as something special - a day they don't want to miss!

Be sure to include several book talks in the days leading up to the library visit. Focus on titles that will help students find new genres or authors they can explore while in the library. During reading conferences discuss the student's current reading selection and encourage them to think about their next book. Don't forget about the TBR list students are using! Encourage students to review their To Be Read lists and mark the titles they are eager to find during the library visit.

Build excitement for the library visit by being excited yourself. Remember many students never get the opportunity to visit a library unless they go with their class at school. Make library days fun and exciting! By having library days with your class, you are providing equitable access to books and resources, increasing equity in literacy.

Make the most of library days by having a selection of books at students' fingertips! Work with the librarian (or library aide) to have several books out on tables or showcased on the bookshelves to make access to relevant titles that much easier. Leverage this time with the librarian. Ask them to interact with your class, make recommendations, and share their favorite books. You may even be able to get them to do a few book talks before letting students browse around.

In addition to allowing students to simply browse the shelves, library days give the teacher the opportunity to match students with books and suggest new authors or styles of writing a student may enjoy in a way that can't be done in the classroom setting.

Once each of your students have found their *just right* book, end your library day with time for students to simply read their new books. Build on the excitement students have for their book choice by providing them with independent reading time.

By scheduling regular library days, teachers unlock the potential for students to discover a world of exciting new stories and authors! Whether it's just once per month or more often, school libraries provide an opportunity for each reader to find that *just right* book! That book that will reignite their motivation for reading.

## *Establish Reading Routines in the Classroom*

Establishing reading routines creates a sense of structure that reduces stress and anxiety for students. These routines will not only help students develop self-discipline, increase their focus, and create a positive learning environment, but it also reduces behavioral problems and provides consistency in instruction. When students understand what is expected of them, they are better able to focus on reading instead of worrying about what they are supposed to do. In this way, establishing routines can improve student motivation for reading.

Classroom routines help promote self-discipline for improved reading habits by providing a consistent, organized framework for reading instruction. When students can anticipate the activities of the day, this helps them take ownership of their learning and encourages them to focus on the task at hand – reading. Having a routine for reading instruction also makes it easier for teachers to monitor student progress and provide the necessary feedback.

Establishing routines helps to increase student focus by providing structure and stability. By establishing expectations for behavior, activities, and transitions in the classroom, students are able to settle into the reading routine quickly, saving precious class time. Routines also help motivate students to stay engaged with their reading because routines provide a sense of safety and security. When students feel safe, they are more likely to stay focused on their books.

Creating consistent reading routines helps reinforce the importance of reading, cultivates good reading habits and ensures students understand the skills they need to become successful readers. Not only can establishing reading routines help create positive reading habits but it also ensures students are getting enough reading practice to ensure a solid foundation for reading skills development.

Things to consider when establishing routines:

- Spend time everyday reading - this could be their independent book or articles needed for class.
- Provide ample opportunities for students to practice their reading skills in meaningful ways through projects or assignments.
- Model good reading behaviors and practices.
- Read aloud as often as possible - students need to hear good fluency in order to develop good fluency.
- Incorporate literacy activities into the daily routine - include literacy skills in your warm ups and closing activities.
- Encourage students to share their thoughts, feelings, and reflections about what they have read, either in writing or through peer discussions.
- Monitor student progress to ensure they are meeting goals and understanding the material.
- Hold students accountable for their reading progress and include them in the monitoring process.
- Make reading a fun and engaging activity for everyone in the classroom!

Routines form habits which is why it is so critical that teachers intentionally make time for reading every day. When students come to class, they should be able to predict that the first fifteen minutes of class is dedicated reading time (or you may choose to read at the end, or for a longer period but it should be consistent) and that every student is expected to have a book and read.

Being able to predict when they will be reading in class also eliminates much of the "I left my book at home." or "I didn't know I needed to bring my book today." distractions which can be a source of frustration for teachers and students alike.

Establishing reading routines in the classroom can help create a positive learning environment for students and foster good reading habits. These routines should provide structure and consistency to ensure students are getting the instruction and time they need to become successful readers. Routines should include ample opportunities for students to practice their reading skills in meaningful ways, provide modeling of good reading habits and practices, and hold students accountable for their reading progress. By establishing consistent routines, teachers can ensure students are developing the skills necessary to become proficient readers.

## *Independent Reading*

In addition to providing students with access to books, teachers must also set aside time for independent reading. If we know that students become better readers if they read more, then teachers must make it a priority to incorporate independent reading in their regular classroom routines. Teachers have to create a class structure that values giving students time to read their choice books.

If teachers don't provide students with time in class to read, many will never pick up a book. Many students don't have time after school to read due to the responsibilities they have at home. We want to show students there is value in reading by giving them time to read during the school day.

Dedicated independent reading time encourages students to read for pleasure, which can help develop literacy skills and increase motivation. It provides an opportunity for students to apply the skills they learned during whole or small group lessons to their choice reading. It also allows students to practice reading strategies such as summarizing and making connections between texts, which can help students become better readers and thinkers overall. Reading independently also helps build comprehension, critical thinking, and vocabulary skills which are essential for academic success.

From the start of the school year, it is essential to set expectations for in class reading time. To ensure that every student understands the value of reading and how to make good use of their independent reading time, it's important to lay out expectations from the beginning.

Here are a few common expectations:

- Everyone is required to have a book (ebook or audiobook) and read the entire time.
- Set a specific amount of time for reading so students know when reading time is over. You can easily set a timer or just write the end time on the board. This helps students self monitor their reading time.
- Find a seat and stay seated for the duration of reading time. This means not getting up to get drinks or asking to use the restroom - yes, you can always make exceptions, but having this as a clear expectation will deter most students from asking as a way to get out of class or put off reading. If you allow your students to move seats, sit in the classroom library, or a comfy chair, on the floor, etc..have them pick their seat and then stay there until the end of reading time.

The objective for setting expectations is not to control students but to eliminate distractions so students can focus on reading.

When teachers argue they don't have time in their schedule for independent reading, it could be argued that we don't have time to not provide time for independent reading. Drill and kill doesn't work - simply completing a packet of worksheets, even if related to a book, doesn't encourage students to want to read. Being forced to read a story, article, or book day after day that a student doesn't like will not improve their desire or ability to read. In fact, it could be argued that being forced to read a book you don't connect with, completing multiple tasks, and taking a test to see if you actually read the book, kills students' desire to read.

Rather than thinking of independent reading as eating up class time, think of it as a time for students to focus on what you are teaching. To apply their skills in an authentic way. Use the time to meet with individual students to discuss their reading journey and provide individual support. Ask probing questions that help students think more critically about what they've read. Use the time to make connections between books and content being taught in other classes. Set goals for students to improve reading comprehension, fluency, and skills such as summarizing or predicting.

Simply providing reading time may not be enough to encourage every student to read. While some students may take advantage of this time to read, others may struggle to find books that interest them or may be reluctant to engage with reading in general.

To address this issue, teachers can provide opportunities for students to engage with reading in different ways.

- **Incorporate reading sprints:** These are short bursts of reading time where everyone in the class reads as much as they can for 10 minutes and then they share about what they read.
- **Use a rubric:** While independent reading time should not be graded, a rubric can help students self-monitor how they spent their time during reading.
- **Partner reading:** If you have a reluctant reader, pair them up with a peer reading the same book. They can take turns reading or you can provide them time to discuss the reading at the end of the reading time.
- **Read alouds:** Engaging with literature through read alouds can foster a genuine passion for reading and help build fluency,

vocabulary, and comprehension skills. With read-alouds, teachers become storytellers that bring texts to life!
- **Make it fun**: Incorporate creative activities such as drawing characters or creating artwork related to a book's theme to help make reading more exciting for reluctant readers.

Creating an environment that encourages independent reading is vital for fostering a love of books and improving student motivation. Teachers play a key role by setting clear expectations, offering a variety of ways to engage, and making reading fun. Reading shouldn't feel like a chore but rather an exciting activity that lets students explore characters, practice reading skills, and develop a deeper understanding of the world around them. When we give students time to read at school, we are helping to create lifelong readers.

## *Book Talks*

### Teachers Share Their Love of Reading

Unlocking the keys to student motivation starts with the teacher sharing their love of reading with students. A teacher's enthusiasm for a particular book can be contagious and often sparks an interest in students who may not have taken the opportunity to pick up a particular book. Book talks are a fun way to get students excited about reading and provide them with the opportunity to add titles to their To Be Read list.

A book talk is a short presentation by the teacher that encourages students to read a particular book. It typically consists of the teacher summarizing the plot, discussing the characters and themes of the book, and expressing enthusiasm for why they think it should be read without giving away too much information. These talks offer teachers the chance to introduce students to books they might not normally be exposed to and encourage them to read something new and different. By sharing their enthusiasm for a book, teachers can often pique student curiosity and motivate them to give it a try. For those who may not be motivated by reading on their own, a teacher-led book talk can provide the "hook" that draws them in.

For example, teachers can share engaging anecdotes, pose thought-provoking questions, or highlight exciting aspects of the book that would appeal specifically to their students. Additionally, teachers can demonstrate good reading habits such as paying attention to context clues or using prediction strategies while discussing the text aloud.

Teacher-led book talks are an excellent way for students to get motivated about reading! By discussing books in an enthusiastic manner and demonstrating good reading habits during these discussions, teachers can help spark curiosity amongst their students and show them how enjoyable–and educational–reading really can be!

**Guest Readers**

Having a real-life author or reader come to class to share their own stories and experiences with literature helps students see how meaningful and powerful literature can be. Not only does this give students an opportunity to connect with a real person, but also allows them to see the impact that books can have on people's lives outside the classroom. This can be incredibly inspiring and motivating for students.

Other teachers or staff members can also be guests. Invite them to do a book talk and share their favorite books with your class. When students see the P.E. teacher coming to their ELA class to share a book, they begin to see reading differently. Students should see reading as a free time activity, something that people choose to do outside of academics.

Inviting guests into the classroom can create a learning experience that will stay with students long after the guest leaves. Guests provide exposure to new books, encourages diverse perspectives, and demonstrates the importance of reading. A guest can help students see the value and relevance of reading in their lives.

**Establish a Safe and Comfortable Reading Environment**

When thinking about creating a culture of reading, think of your classroom environment as setting the stage. Is your classroom one that prioritizes reading? Can students find reading materials and then get comfortable and start reading? How students feel about their environment can greatly impact their willingness to engage in reading.

Establishing a safe and comfortable reading environment is just one way you can reengage students in reading. Students should feel respected, supported, and valued. They should feel safe taking risks and learning new things without fear of judgment or criticism. By creating a culture of reading in the classroom, teachers can create an important foundation for students to begin growing as readers.

In addition to building positive, supportive relationships, creating a safe environment is key to inspiring students to engage in reading. Whether that be through special seating, a classroom library full of up to date, relevant books, or access to natural light, all these little details add up to creating a warm atmosphere that invites students to pick up a book and get lost in its pages. Allowing students to sit in a fun chair, a cozy corner, or even something as simple as the opportunity to sit on the floor to read can help create an environment that is more conducive to independent reading.

**Set Expectations for Success**

Show students that reading has value and that you believe in their ability by setting high expectations. Make sure your expectations are clearly communicated to students—be specific about what they should be able to do at each level by the end of the year. Make sure you give regular, honest feedback about their progress, so they feel comfortable coming to you with questions or concerns. This feedback should be constructive and focused on what they should do next rather than dwelling on mistakes made in the past.

Establishing an atmosphere of reading success in the classroom has lifelong consequences for students! By setting clear expectations and providing consistent feedback and support, you can help your students learn to enjoy reading again.

## *Final Thoughts*

1. Giving students ownership over their reading choices is essential for promoting lifelong reading and developing a love of literature.
2. Allowing students to abandon books that don't resonate with them can promote a positive attitude toward reading and create a more inclusive classroom environment.
3. Providing opportunities for students to share their favorite books can inspire a deeper love of reading and promote critical thinking and creativity.
4. Teachers should stock their classroom library with quality books that represent the diversity of their student and community population to create an atmosphere of respect and inclusion.
5. It is more important to have books in the classroom library that students will read than to have a beautiful collection of books that no one will pick up.
6. Establishing reading routines in the classroom can help create a sense of structure that reduces stress and anxiety for students, leading to increased focus and motivation for reading.
7. Dedicated independent reading time allows students to develop literacy skills learned in class and encourages students to read for pleasure.
8. Book talks are opportunities for teachers to share their love of reading with students and motivate them to read new and different books.
9. Having guest readers, such as authors or other teachers, can help students see the value that books have on people's lives and inspire students to read more.
10. By setting clear expectations and providing consistent support, teachers can help students learn to enjoy reading again and establish a lifelong love of reading.

# 3

# Reigniting the Spark

*What we have learned from others becomes our own by reflection. -*
Ralph Waldo Emerson

   In the spring of 2020, our lives were turned upside down and while some were able to continue living with little change other than staying home, for many, their lives became about survival, and rightfully so! The pandemic disrupted traditional education creating large gaps in student learning. Now that students have returned to the classroom, it's time to reignite the spark and get students reading again!
   Chapter 3 offers teachers a fresh perspective on teaching reading in the classroom. This chapter presents ways to innovate the secondary ELA strategies you already know to help rekindle students' love for reading and boost their confidence.
   Each section provides practical ideas for updating traditional methods and adapting to the new normal. By incorporating the techniques outlined in each section, teachers can reach students who may have fallen behind and help close the learning gaps created by the pandemic.
   With the right mindset and tools, teachers can inspire their students to become lifelong learners who enjoy reading for pleasure and

personal growth. This chapter aims to provide educators with guidance and inspiration to motivate students and improve reading skills among their students.

## *Assessing Student's Skill Levels and Needs*

We must first start this conversation by recognizing that students' skills are not at the same level they were prior to the pandemic. Teachers need to be prepared to teach skills that in previous years, they did not have to. This could be anything from teaching phonological awareness to providing more explicit instruction on comprehension strategies. You may find you need to step back and teach a skill two or three grade levels below what you would normally have to in the past in order to reach the grade level objective by the end of your unit. It is no longer one or two students that need this additional support, it is now entire classes or nearly entire classes.

But how do teachers know where to start? How do they assess what level their students are starting from? Traditionally teachers would look at data from the previous year's testing to see what reading level their students are on and use that as their baseline. However, this data has been skewed for the past few years, if it is available at all.

In the following section, we will talk about ways to assess your students if you have no, or limited, data from the previous year.

### District Screeners

Standardized reading screeners are one tool teachers can use to quickly assess where their students are with their reading skills. With the information they provide, teachers can begin the school year on a solid footing and understand which students need more assistance and support. By using a standardized screener, teachers can determine which students will need more one-on-one instruction or small group activities to help make improvements in their students' reading abilities.

Screeners can provide a benchmark for measuring student progress throughout the school year. Each time the teacher administers the screener, they can measure student growth and adjust instruction accordingly. It is important to remember that standardized screeners are just a snapshot of students' abilities and should not be used as the only method of assessing students.

Ideally, your district will provide a reading screener you can use throughout the year. If your district does not provide a screener, it is important to take informal assessments and observations at the beginning of the year to see where students are starting. You will find that pre-assessing students on specific skills will give you the data you need in order to best meet them where they are.

## Informal Observations

Informal observation is an effective way for teachers to assess their students' reading abilities. Teachers can observe their students during class discussions, independent reading time, and during reading conferences. By doing so, they can get a sense of each student's reading level, decoding skills, fluency, and comprehension abilities.

Observing students during independent reading time can provide insight into their reading interests and level of engagement with the text. During reading conferences, teachers should ask students to read a paragraph or two out loud which allows the teacher to assess fluency, accuracy, and the student's decoding skills. Teachers can also observe how their students approach unfamiliar words and passages, and identify areas where they may need additional support. Additionally, teachers can observe how their students interact with the text and make inferences, predictions, and connections.

It is important for teachers to use informal observation as a complement to formal assessments. While standardized screeners provide valuable data, they do not capture the full picture of each student's reading abilities. By combining formal assessments with informal observations, teachers can gain a more complete understanding of each student's strengths and areas for growth.

Informal observations also allow teachers to differentiate instruction to better meet the needs of each student. By identifying areas where students struggle, teachers can provide targeted support and instruction. Additionally, observation can help teachers identify students who may benefit from additional interventions or support services.

### Reader Interest Surveys and Ongoing Reflections

Surveys are a great way for teachers to get an initial sense of their students' reading history and how they feel about reading overall. Surveys can provide teachers with the opportunity to find out what type of books their students prefer, if they can self-identify any difficulties they have with reading, or anything else that might be helpful when addressing the needs of the student.

Additionally, surveys can help teachers get a better understanding of each student's individual interest and attitude about reading. For example, a survey could ask about what genres the student finds engaging or what types of books they enjoy (novels, graphic novels, books written in verse, etc..). Surveys can also give the teacher insight into how much time the student spends reading both in and out of class. By being able to identify these elements, teachers can then use this information to better meet the needs of each individual student.

Surveys are a good activity to do at the beginning of the year but consider having students complete another survey around mid-year to see how students' attitudes about reading have changed (or not). The midyear survey is a great way for both teachers and students to reflect on their progress.

## *Strategies for Reengagement*

Reading is an important part of a student's educational journey, and unlocking the keys to motivation can make a significant difference in student success both now and long term. With this in mind, there are many creative ways to encourage students to fall in love with reading. This section will explore a variety of strategies to help teachers foster a love of reading with their students.

Before we get into specific strategies, let's take a moment to recognize again that what students are able to do now is different from what they could do prepandemic. The suggestions that follow are not meant to dumb down the curriculum or decrease expectations for learning, but are meant to encourage teachers to meet students where they are and then build them up from there. This may require taking a step back and teaching skills or processes you didn't need to teach a few years ago. That doesn't mean that anything is wrong or students aren't making progress; it is simply a recognition that skill levels are different and students have gaps in their learning.

It will take time, but student abilities will recover if teachers invest the time now to meet the needs of students. Give yourself permission to slow down when you need to and do what is right for the students in your class.

If we don't acknowledge students need more academic support than ever before and continue pushing forward like nothing has happened, just hoping students will magically catch up, we are at a real threat of widening the gap even more - to a point we may never recover.

Teachers have to be okay with teaching things they deem to be below grade level because that is where students' learning gaps are. That doesn't mean teachers need to throw out everything they have done in the past. Things such as student choice, graphic organizers, book clubs, and the like don't have to be eliminated. Instead, how teachers implement these practices needs to be adjusted to match the skill level and abilities of the students in their classes today.

This is easier said than done when districts and administration want to return to business as usual. It is unfair that they continually tie the hands of educators by punishing them with bad yearly reviews or write-ups if they are not teaching grade level standards. They should understand that sometimes you have to teach or reteach standards that students haven't mastered or were skipped because of the modified curriculum of the past few years. A good administration will understand, acknowledge, and support these efforts.

The strategies discussed in this section are meant to help teachers reshape their approach to meet the needs of students. While some strategies and ideas may not be new, it's important to remember that they can serve as a starting point for brainstorming how to tweak them to best meet the needs of students.

## Student Interest

Student engagement is an essential part of learning. Finding ways to incorporate choices and activities based on student interest can help reignite the spark for reading.

Choice reading is one way to bring student interest into the classroom. Allowing students to choose books related to topics they have already learned about or topics they want to learn more about will increase the likelihood they will engage with the book. This helps pique their curiosity, as well as increase their understanding of concepts covered earlier in class. For example, if a group of students enjoys studying ancient Rome, why not let them explore some historical fiction books or books based on Roman mythology? If a student has expressed an interest in animals – let them explore non-fiction books written by experts on different types of mammals! See chapter 2 for more information on choice reading.

Teachers should think about the tasks they are asking students to complete and the books they are asking students to read. How many of those were created based on student interest? Of course, not every assignment or task can be designed around student interest; there simply isn't enough time in the day to plan that many activities for every student! But as often as you can, incorporate activities that connect with student interests.

## Connect New Learning with Stories Students Already Know

The best way to help students learn is by making learning fun and engaging. One way to do this is to tie new concepts or skills to stories students already know. This helps to bring back nostalgic memories from when students first encountered the story, which in turn makes it easier for them to engage in the new learning because they already know the story.

When teachers use familiar stories as part of their instructional strategy, the stress of comprehending a new text is taken away, allowing the student to focus on learning the new skill. For example, when teaching summarizing skills, use a story such as *Cinderella* or *Charlie and the Chocolate Factory*. By starting with a story students are familiar with, teachers can focus on teaching how to summarize without worrying whether students understood the text.

Once students understand the new skill, they can then apply it to their own choice reading books. If a student struggles to apply the skill on their own, the teacher can easily follow up during reading conferences where they can clarify or reteach, if needed.

By linking students' past reading experiences with current instruction, teachers create a learning environment that focuses on the mastery of skills. It allows the students to focus on the skill without getting bogged down with comprehension.

**Make Thinking Visible for Students**

There's nothing more frustrating for a student than not knowing how they are supposed to complete a task. As a secondary teacher it is easy to take for granted the idea that students come to class already knowing how to think and problem solve, and in years past teachers would help students develop and refine those skills, but in today's education environment, teachers need to explicitly teach these skills.

It isn't that teachers were ignoring these skills during the pandemic, but circumstances such as online teaching, modified standards, shortened school days, and the like made it so these skills did not get the same attention they had in previous years. The result: students are returning to the classroom not knowing how to think academically for themselves. They missed out on much of the modeling and practice that would have set them up for the rigor of secondary ELA.

For this reason, it has become increasingly important for teachers to make thinking visible in the classroom. By making thinking visible, students learn how to approach problems, analyze texts and interpret data - all skills that are essential for success in secondary ELA and beyond.

This section will discuss strategies that can be used to make thinking visible and help students understand how they should be approaching their learning. When students know what to do, it increases their confidence which will impact their motivation to complete the assigned tasks.

**Modeling**: Modeling what you expect students to be able to do is not a new concept, but, due to the extraordinary circumstances teachers faced in 2020 and into 2021, students missed out on much of the visual aspect of learning. Because so much of the modeling disappeared when schools went to emergency online teaching, it is even more important now that teachers model for students not only behavior expectations but model how they approach reading.

Modeling is one of the most effective methods for showing students how they can approach their own reading. It allows students to be able to see how a teacher decides what to read, how they stay engaged with the story and when they know it is time to abandon a book and find a new one. Modeling can also help build students' confidence as they feel more secure in their ability to complete the task.

Teachers should also model what it looks like to read in the classroom. Create an anchor chart with examples of what independent reading time looks like and sounds like. This will help students understand what the reading environment looks like in an academic setting.

**Think-Alouds**: Think-Alouds are an important teaching tool for students as they help students understand the thought process of their teacher in real time. A think aloud is when the teacher reads a text out loud pausing to verbally demonstrate what they are thinking about as they read. By thinking out loud, teachers are able to show students how they make connections between ideas, how they solve problems, and how they approach reading when it gets difficult. This provides students with a valuable opportunity to observe and learn from the teacher's own thought process.

For example, when teaching a new concept, the teacher should demonstrate their thinking by pausing periodically and thinking out loud specifically about the skill they are teaching - teach the student how to think about the skill as they read. The teacher might explain how to break down complex words into simpler parts when encountering unfamiliar words within a text. By doing this, students can more easily replicate their teacher's thought process and apply it to their own reading.

**Graphic Organizers**: Graphic organizers are a great visual tool for students. They are particularly effective in helping students understand complex concepts by providing a way to visually break down information into easy to understand chunks. Organizers give students the ability to think through a text on their own. As they complete the graphic organizer, they have to process what they read to determine which facts are most important and how they are related. This helps to solidify their understanding of the material.

For example, a teacher might present a graphic organizer in the form of a Venn diagram to help students compare and contrast two different authors' views on a particular topic. The teacher could have the students write the main point of each argument at the top of either half of the diagram and then ask them to fill in details underneath that support their claims. This would allow students to clearly see how each author's view differs and what similarities exist between them.

Graphic organizers provide an excellent structure for analyzing or summarizing material and can be used to identify themes, create summaries, or even organize information. These visual representations help students think more critically about the material and make connections between concepts that may be difficult to explain with words alone. In short, graphic organizers allow students to visualize their understanding of a topic in a way that is both easy for them to follow and leads to independent thinking.

## Stations

Stations are not just for elementary classrooms! Station activities are a fun and engaging way to differentiate instruction, and provide more practice, as well as, review skills. Not only do stations provide students with multiple opportunities for success, they also allow for movement, give students autonomy to work at their own pace, and can be used to cover more content in a smaller amount of time.

When teachers offer differentiated learning methods, they provide multiple opportunities for students to be successful. Each station can focus on specific skills, so teachers can provide more targeted instruction than if all students were working on the same skill or task at once. This makes it easier to reteach or reinforce skills and provides differentiated opportunities for learning which keeps students motivated.

Stations give students flexibility and control over their learning experience by allowing them to move around the classroom as they work independently or collaboratively. Stations allow students to have choice in what task they do first or which station they go to next. This alone increases engagement because students have a sense of control which ultimately helps them take ownership over their learning. Station work can help break up long periods of sitting without having to stop instruction for a break. Giving students opportunities to move helps keep their energy high and their attention focused on learning.

Station activities are an efficient way for teachers to cover more material within a shorter amount of time since all the students are working on different tasks simultaneously. This means that teachers can cover more content than they could if they had stayed with a traditional lesson plan where each student moves through the curriculum at the same time.

## Small Groups

Small groups are another strategy that you typically see in elementary classrooms but can be just as effective in secondary ELA. Small group instruction is an effective way to provide focused instruction to a specific group of students, teaching them the skills they need to grow academically.

Small-group instruction offers numerous benefits - from personalized instruction to improved collaboration amongst peers, students are getting what they need when they need it. There are many ways you can group your students.

**Grouping By Strategy/Skill:** When you want to focus on a specific skill or strategy with students, strategy groups are a good option. This type of group allows teachers to provide instruction on specific topics that are relevant for each student.

Grouping by strategy allows the teacher to differentiate instruction based on student needs of a specific skill. Some students may need additional support just one time and other students may need more support meeting in a strategy small group multiple times. All students in a strategy group are working towards mastery of the same skill.

**Interest Groups**: Interest groups provide an excellent opportunity for small group reading activities based on a shared interest. By finding texts that all students in the group can relate to and enjoy, teachers will create a learning environment that encourages engagement with academic tasks - like basketball fans devouring the pages of their favorite sport-centered book! Working in these smaller settings helps inspire motivation and enthusiasm while developing key literacy skills.

Students are engaged in the group because they enjoy the topic. Their motivation is high because they have a connection to the content. When conducting small groups based on interest, teachers can group multiple abilities together creating a great opportunity for students to learn and collaborate together.

**Grouping By Ability**: Grouping by ability is especially helpful when the goal is for all of your students to reach mastery of certain concepts or skills. Grouping by ability allows you to tailor instruction according to each student's level so they can move through the curriculum at a rate that works best for them without feeling overwhelmed.

Using small-group instruction in secondary ELA classrooms, teachers help foster engagement with academic tasks, motivate and inspire students, and allow students to progress at their own pace. With careful planning and consideration of these strategies, you can create an equitable learning environment that leads to student growth.

## Reading Conferences

Reading conferences are motivating for students because they provide an opportunity for a one-on-one discussion with their teacher. Reading conferences are brief conversations between the teacher and student about the student's comprehension of their choice reading material.

During a reading conference, the teacher asks open-ended questions that allow the student to share what they know and understand about their book and how they have applied the reading skills being taught in class. It is also a chance for teachers to recognize areas where the student has made progress, and identify and target any areas of difficulty.

As the teacher and student discuss progress, they create goals the student will focus on. It is the goal setting during each conference that helps give students a sense of ownership, giving them something to work towards and encouraging a growth mindset. Reading conferences are an opportunity for students to feel heard and valued as readers, knowing that their teacher cares about their progress and wants to see them succeed.

**Reading Reflections Not Reading Logs**

Reading reflections provide teachers with a valuable tool to hold students accountable for their reading while also providing students with an opportunity to think about what they have read. Unlike traditional reading logs which only require students to tally up the number of pages read, reading reflections offer students an opportunity to engage in meaningful reflection and discussion about their book.

A reading reflection is an activity in which students read choice books then actively reflect on what they've read. Through reflective writing or verbal conversations, students are able to express their thoughts, impressions, interpretations and connections to the text. It also encourages students to think deeply about the implications the text has for their own lives and ask questions that help them gain further insights into its meaning.

Reading reflections can be more motivating than simply counting pages because it helps promote personal growth and allows students to make meaningful connections with the text they are reading. Furthermore, it provides an opportunity for students to not only comprehend complex information effectively but also express themselves creatively by generating their own interpretations of the material. By engaging in this type of exercise, students are able to sharpen their analytical skills and become more invested in what they are reading. It is an activity that encourages students to develop a deeper understanding of the material and provides them with a much richer experience than simply counting pages.

By introducing reflections in place of reading logs, teachers can be confident that their students are understanding and appropriately applying the content skills they have learned. Additionally, it gives teachers a better understanding of where each student is with their reading and allows them to provide targeted support when needed. Ultimately, reading reflections offer an alternative to traditional reading logs and can help students practice skills, demonstrate what they know, and become more invested in reading.

## Peer-to-Peer Conversations

Peer-to-peer conversations are important for motivating students because conversations allow students to discuss their favorite topics, books, authors, and the genres that excite them. Having an opportunity to explain why a book is meaningful to them and then hearing what their peers think about it can be very motivating for students. When students engage in authentic conversations with peers, they often share about things they are interested in which can help them develop a deeper understanding of the book. This helps students begin to see reading as something not just for school, but something enjoyable they can share with others.

Peer-to-peer conversations also provide opportunities for students to practice their reading comprehension skills, as they have to think critically about the book and explain it in detail. Discussions between peers gives students the opportunity to hear different perspectives on the topic, allowing them to gain new insights into the story. Additionally, by engaging in peer discussions, students learn how to communicate effectively with one another which is an important life skill in itself.

It can sometimes be difficult to get students to open up and share with one other. This section will offer ideas to get students interacting with peers and talking about the books they are reading so they can better express their ideas to each other.

## Partner Talks

If peer-to-peer conversations are new to you, start slow and incorporate what you can, including more conversations when students are ready. A great place to start is after independent reading, simply have students share with a partner what they have just read. By starting with these small conversations, you are creating a safe space for everyone's opinions to be heard, making it more likely that students will engage in discussions.

As you begin incorporating partner talks, be sure to set expectations for students and model how conversations should be conducted. This could include explaining the importance of respectful dialogue, staying on task, and listening to one another. It may also be helpful to provide students with several sentence starters to help initiate conversations. Sentence starters can encourage more elaborate dialogues as well as foster critical thinking skills. Sentence starter examples could include, "I noticed that ___" or "I found it interesting when ___ happened." These types of open-ended questions can lead to deeper discussions.

Once students are comfortable with partner talks, take the next step to include student-led book talks or even venture into book clubs.

## Student-Led Book Talks

Student-led book talks encourage students to engage in conversations about literature while also motivating them to explore reading material that interests them. Student-led book talks are similar to teacher book talks discussed in Chapter 2, however with student-led book talks, students are at the center of the conversation. Students get the opportunity to share their thoughts, ideas, and experiences with a book with their peers.

Book talks can be done as a whole group, but they are best when done in small groups. Students are more likely to engage in conversation when the groups are smaller and it's less likely that one or two students will dominate the conversation.

During a book talk, a student provides an overview of the plot and their analysis of why they enjoyed or didn't enjoy certain elements of the book. They come to the group with stories and questions and seek out the opinions of their peers. After each presentation, other members of the group provide feedback or ask questions before the group moves on to the next student.

This form of discussion helps students connect with what they read and students see a purpose in reading beyond just a task assigned by their teacher. This promotes student ownership over their learning experience, which in turn helps them see the value in what they are doing. Book talks are a fun way for students to share their enthusiasm and knowledge about books with one another!

## Book Clubs

A book club is a small group of students who come together to read and discuss a book they have all read - ideally one they have chosen to read. It differs from a student-led book talk in that everyone in a book club reads the same book. It is an opportunity for students to explore literature in a collaborative environment where everyone brings their own unique perspectives and interpretations.

During a book club meeting, students discuss the plot, characters, theme, and other literary elements. They also pose questions or provide critiques of how certain elements were represented in the book. Through collaborative discussions, students explore the meaning of the text beyond the words on the page. They work together to solve problems and build empathy for others.

In order to make the most of book clubs, it is important for teachers to set clear expectations and create an atmosphere that encourages meaningful dialogue. By doing this, teachers can provide students with a safe space where ideas flow freely. It is this sense of community that makes book clubs so motivating for students.

When structured in the right way, book club discussions become fun, productive learning experiences that help foster critical thinking as well as the development of important literacy and life skills.

Overall, book clubs are an excellent tool for developing a student's literary analysis skills, promoting reading comprehension, and fostering meaningful conversations about literature. Book clubs also provide students with an opportunity to explore new books and engage in thoughtful discussions with their peers. By creating an environment in which students can share their own interpretations and opinions, book clubs help foster a greater appreciation for literature.

## Mini Blogging

Not all peer-to-peer interactions need to be verbal. For teachers looking for a quieter, more controlled way to encourage peer-to-peer discussions, try mini blogging. Mini blogging is essentially the same as silent conversations, however, the student creates a written piece before sharing it with their peers. This activity can be done on paper or digitally.

Mini blogging is just like regular blogging except it focuses on shorter posts related to a book a student is currently reading. Mini blogging allows the teacher to assign a specific topic or task such as "Explain how the events in your book change how the main character sees the world," or let students choose their own topics to write about as it relates to their reading.

Once the students have written their blog posts, they should share them with their classmates and participate in a silent conversation. Students read the posts written by other student's and provide feedback through comments or questions. This can be done in multiple ways such as adding comments to the actual blog, responding on an online forum, or by writing a response on paper or sticky notes.

There are several benefits of mini blogging in addition to getting your students excited about reading. It is the perfect way to let your introverted students shine. It encourages peer-to-peer conversations which give students an opportunity to practice their communication skills and build relationships with one another. Mini blogging holds students accountable for their reading as they are required to think critically and creatively about what they have read and communicate that understanding with others. Finally, by sharing their mini blog posts with the class, it will help foster a sense of community as everyone has something unique and meaningful to contribute.

## *Productive Struggle*

When it comes to teaching in general, productive struggle is a critical component. It's a concept that many teachers shy away from, but one that can have huge implications for student learning, student confidence, and student motivation. Productive struggle is the idea of allowing students to work through difficult tasks with limited adult intervention. This practice allows students to develop problem-solving skills and confidence, and to learn to think deeply about a task.

Being able to productively struggle means that a student has the ability to think critically and independently when faced with a challenge. This type of independent thinking helps students develop confidence in their own skills and abilities, which have long-term benefits in terms of academic success. Learning that it is okay to not have the answer right away, and to productively struggle to find their own solution, encourages students to be creative problem solvers—which is something they can use throughout thier life.

Productive struggle also provides teachers with valuable information about a student's understanding of the material. The amount of time it takes for a student to complete a task or the types of errors they make can provide insight into areas that need further instruction or clarification. This type of feedback is invaluable for teachers as it allows them to tailor their instruction to meet the needs of their students.

Productive struggle is hard because teachers want to see every student succeed. So the tendency is to jump in too fast and rescue the student from the struggle. However, if teachers don't allow students the opportunity to productively struggle, we rob students of the ability to develop the skills needed to be independent thinkers and problem solvers. What we inadvertently end up teaching them is if they wait, someone else will do the thinking for them.

Productive struggle is not leaving students to fend for themselves when the work becomes too difficult. Rather it is providing some guidance then allowing the student to do the thinking, the trial and error, and the final reassessing of their thinking which leads them to the desired outcome. Teachers must step in to provide the teaching, the modeling, and the resources the students need, but then provide the wait time needed to give students a chance to work through the struggle on their own.

Part of learning is being willing to take risks and, if teachers want students to feel comfortable with risk taking, teachers have to get comfortable with students not succeeding the first time they try something new. In an effort to make things better and decrease student stress due to the trauma of the pandemic, we have taught students that if they wait long enough, the teacher will give them the answer. Teachers have forgotten that productive struggle is a good thing. When students are faced with a challenge, we want to encourage them to think through the situation, problem solve and find the solution on their own. We don't want them to give up or simply wait for the answer.

Productive struggle and risk taking are what lead to growth and the ability of students to apply the skills they are learning. It teaches students that mistakes are a part of the learning process and that it is okay to make them. It is through taking risks and experiencing challenges that students can develop the skills necessary to succeed academically and in their future careers. It is the role of the educator to foster a classroom culture that supports productive struggle and encourages students to embrace the journey of learning, mistakes and all!

## *Final Thoughts*

1. The pandemic has caused significant disruptions in student learning, particularly in reading skills, and teachers need to adapt their teaching strategies to address the gaps.
2. It may be necessary to teach skills that are two or three grade levels below what would typically be expected.
3. Formal assessments and informal observations should be used together to gain a more complete understanding of each student's strengths and areas for growth in reading.
4. Acknowledge that student abilities are different than before the pandemic and adjust teaching methods accordingly.
5. Make thinking visible for students by explicitly teaching problem-solving and critical thinking skills.
6. Reading conferences provide an opportunity for one-on-one discussions between teachers and students, where teachers can ask open-ended questions to assess student comprehension and progress, set goals, and encourage a growth mindset.
7. Reading reflections are motivating and provide a rich experience

for students, allowing them to sharpen their analytical skills and become more invested in reading.
8. Peer-to-peer conversations are important for motivating students. The provide opportunities for students to discuss topics, books, authors, and genres that excite them.
9. Productive struggle is a critical component of teaching that can have huge implications for student learning, confidence, and motivation.
10. Mistakes are a part of the learning process, and it is essential to foster a classroom culture that supports productive struggle and encourages students to embrace the journey of learning.

# 4

# Motivation through Goal Setting

*When it is obvious that the goals cannot be reached, don't adjust the goals, adjust the action step.* - Confucius

Goal setting involves helping each student identify their individual strengths and then finding ways to apply those strengths towards achieving specific goals related to reading. Teachers can start by encouraging students to think about their long-term academic goals and then work backward in order to set smaller, achievable goals.

It's important for teachers to help students break down these goals into smaller steps so they don't become overwhelmed or discouraged. The key here is for educators to provide guidance while still allowing students the autonomy they need for self-motivation and self-efficacy to grow over time.

Goal setting is a critical component of learning that is often overlooked by students when it comes to academic success. Setting goals is a powerful tool that can help students focus their efforts, stay motivated, and achieve their dreams. When students set academic goals, they are essentially creating a roadmap for their own academic journey, identifying the steps they need to take to reach their desired destination.

In this chapter, we will explore the importance of goal setting with students and discuss how it benefits their academic success.

## *Types of Goals*

### Independent reading goals

Encouraging students to set their own reading goals and track their progress can be a powerful way to promote independent reading and improve reading skills. When students set their own reading goals, they take ownership of their learning and become more engaged in the reading process.

Students should set achievable goals based on their reading level, interests, and available time. Students can set goals for the number of books they want to read, the number of pages they want to read each day, or the amount of time they want to spend reading each week. To support student-led reading goals, teachers can provide guidance and resources, such as reading logs or trackers, to help students monitor their own progress.

Once students have set their goals, they can track their progress using a reading log or tracker. These tools can be helpful for students when monitoring their own progress. Refrain from setting reading goals that all students must achieve (ie. read 250 pages each week) in the same amount of time. There are many factors that go into a students' ability to read. It is not equitable to assume that all students can read a specific number of pages in the same time period even if they are reading at their own level.

The trackers will help students be accountable for their own reading goals while also providing them with a sense of accomplishment as they see their progress over time. Teachers can provide feedback and support to help students adjust their goals when needed, based on individual progress and student needs.

By promoting student-led reading goals and helping students track their own progress, teachers can help students develop important skills such as self-motivation, self-direction, and goal setting. Student-led reading goals can foster a love of reading that lasts a lifetime, while also providing students with the skills and knowledge they need to succeed academically.

### Comprehension Goals

Comprehension goals are designed to help students improve their ability to understand and interpret the meaning of a text. These goals focus on developing students' skills in identifying the main ideas and details of a text, making inferences, drawing conclusions, and identifying the author's purpose among other things.

Students should set goals that focus on specific reading strategies, such as summarizing, predicting, questioning, or visualizing in order to develop comprehension skills. Teachers should also provide opportunities for students to practice these skills through guided reading, independent reading, and class discussions.

### Vocabulary Goals

Vocabulary goals are designed to help students expand their vocabulary which will help them comprehend more complex texts. These goals focus on developing students' skills in learning new words, understanding their meanings, and using them appropriately in context.

Understanding the meanings of words is also an important aspect of reading comprehension. Students should set goals related to looking up the definitions of new words online or being able to use context clues.

To help students achieve their vocabulary goals, teachers can provide multiple opportunities to practice new words. Utilizing such things as word walls, games, and other resources will encourage students to practice their newly acquired words. Teachers can also model the use of new words in their own speaking and writing, and encourage students to ask questions and seek clarification when they encounter unfamiliar words.

By setting vocabulary goals, students will improve their communication skills and become better readers. A strong vocabulary is essential for academic success.

**Genre Goals**

Encouraging students to read a variety of genres is an important component of promoting literacy. By setting genre goals, students will expand their reading horizons, broaden their understanding of the world, and develop a diverse range of reading interests.

To set genre goals, teachers can provide students with a list of genres and encourage them to select the genres they are most interested in exploring. Students can set goals for the number of books or articles they want to read in each genre, or for the amount of time they want to spend reading in each genre.

Setting genre goals can help students develop a wide range of reading skills, such as identifying literary elements and analyzing texts. It can also help students broaden their knowledge and understanding of different cultures, historical events, and social issues.

By setting genre goals, students can become more engaged and motivated in their reading, while also developing a lifelong love of learning. By providing students with opportunities to explore different genres and share their reading experiences with each other, teachers can help students develop important social and emotional skills such as empathy, collaboration, and communication. Ultimately, genre goals can help students become well-rounded, thoughtful readers who are equipped with the skills and knowledge they need to succeed academically and beyond.

These are just a few examples of the types of goals students can set for themselves. Goals can be set for any skill students want or need to improve. The main thing to keep in mind is the goal must be attainable, reasonable for learning, and personalized to the student.

## *Set Achievable Goals*

When students begin to set their goals, it is important that the teacher work with the student to ensure the goals they set are actually attainable. Students are more likely to be successful with big goals if the smaller goals are realistic and attainable. There is nothing wrong with helping students meet several smaller goals on their way to one really large goal.

For example, if a student sets a goal to read one hour each night but has not opened a book all year, that probably will not be the best goal for that student to start with. Encourage the student to write a more realistic goal. Maybe have them start with simply reading each night - that can be 10 minutes or an hour but start with the goal of reading every night. Once they reach that goal, work with the student to read for 30 minutes a night, then 45 minutes, and so on until the student's original goal is met.

Students often believe they have one shot to hit their goal and can easily shut down if they don't meet the goal on the first try. Encourage students by reminding them that failures (setbacks) are simply part of the process. If they don't achieve their goal right away, help them reflect on the actions they took to meet the goal. Teachers should help students evaluate if they need to break the goal down further, if the student needs more instruction in a particular area or if the student just needs to give themselves some grace and start again.

## *Involve Students in the Goal-Setting Process*

The first step in creating reading goals is helping students identify their own individual strengths and find ways to use those strengths in their goal setting. In Chapter 2 we discussed using a screener to help identify student strengths and weaknesses in reading. Don't be afraid to share those results with students.

When framed in a way that showcases what students are able to do and identifies only one or two areas students can focus on, sharing the results of the screener is beneficial. It is not suggested to simply show students their grade level equivalency in reading and let them decide their goals from that - this leaves students often feeling overwhelmed and defeated.

Involving students in the goal-setting process will help bring meaning to the goal for the student. Students should be able to identify skills by name and have an understanding of what they are working towards before they set goals. After all, if students don't understand what they are working towards, their goals are just words.

Involving students in the goal setting process also...

- **Increases motivation and engagement**: When students are involved in setting their own goals, they feel a sense of ownership and investment in their learning. This can lead to increased motivation and engagement in the learning process, as students are more likely to be invested in achieving goals they helped set.
- **Develops a growth mindset**: Involving students in the goal-setting process can help them develop a growth mindset, which is the belief that their abilities can be developed through hard work and dedication. This can help students overcome challenges and persevere in the face of setbacks.
- **Improves academic performance**: Setting goals and monitoring progress can help students identify areas where they need to improve and take steps to address those areas. This can lead to improved academic performance and greater confidence in their abilities.
- **Develops self-regulation skills**: Goal-setting requires students to develop self-regulation skills such as planning, monitoring their progress, and making adjustments as needed. These skills are important for academic success and are also transferable to other areas of life, such as work and personal relationships.
- **Improves communication and collaboration skills**: When students are involved in the goal-setting process, they have opportunities to communicate with their teachers and peers about their goals and progress. This can help them develop important

communication and collaboration skills essential for success in school and beyond.

Overall, involving students in the goal-setting process can help them become more self-directed and motivated learners. By providing opportunities for students to set and achieve their own goals, teachers can help students become more confident and successful in all areas of their lives.

## *Help Students Monitor Their Progress*

To help students achieve their reading goals, it's important for teachers to create opportunities for students to monitor their own progress. One effective way to do this is through weekly reflections or during reading conferences. Checklists and rubrics can also be helpful tools to ensure students know exactly what they need to do to reach their goals.

Monitoring their own progress is a new skill for many students in secondary ELA. Students are used to turning in assignments and receiving feedback from the teacher with little to no input. However, it is important for students to take ownership of their learning and be able to monitor their own progress if we want to see them achieve long term goals. Teachers can train students on how to monitor their progress over time with tools like checklists and rubrics.

By monitoring their own progress, students can make adjustments as needed and take pride in their accomplishments when they reach their goals. This helps them to build confidence and a sense of responsibility for their own learning.

## **Intrinsic vs Extrinsic Motivation**

Although intrinsic motivation is the ultimate goal for every teacher to instill in their students, not all students are ready to engage in learning solely for the sake of learning. As a result, many teachers resort to using an extrinsic reward system as a way to motivate their students -

providing treats or prizes in exchange for completing tasks. While this can be effective in the short term, it can create problems down the road because you are conditioning students to work only if they receive a reward.

On the other hand, when students have the freedom to choose what they read and learn, they are more motivated to engage in it because they have a personal investment in the learning. This personal investment leads to authentic learning experiences that are more meaningful and relevant to students' lives.

Think back to your own college experience. You likely had a class or two that didn't interest you, but you persevered because you were working towards a degree - something you valued. Giving students the freedom to choose promotes intrinsic motivation, which ultimately leads to increased overall motivation, greater engagement, and better success in the learning process.

## Strategies for Students Monitoring Progress

There are several ways that students can monitor their own progress toward achieving their reading goals. Here are some examples:

> **Keep a reading log**: Students can keep a log of the books they have read, the pages they have completed, or the time they have spent reading. This log can be used to track their progress over time and set new goals as they reach milestones.
>
> **Use checklists or rubrics**: Checklists or rubrics can be used to help students understand what is expected of them in terms of their reading goals. They can use these tools to track their progress and identify areas where they need to improve.
>
> **Reflect on their reading**: Students can reflect on their reading on a regular basis, such as weekly or after finishing a book. They can ask themselves questions such as, "What did I learn from this book?" or "What do I still need to work on?" This

reflection can help students understand their strengths and weaknesses and set new goals accordingly.

**Discuss progress during reading conferences**: During reading conferences, teachers can have conversations with students about their reading progress. They can ask students about the books they have read, what they liked or didn't like about them, and how they feel about their progress toward their goals. This is a valuable opportunity for students to reflect on their progress and get feedback to understand if they are meeting their goal or how they should modify their goal to make it more attainable.

By using these methods, students can monitor their own progress toward their reading goals and take ownership of their learning. This can help them become more motivated and engaged learners.

## *Celebrate Successes Along the Way*

When your students reach the goals that they have set for themselves, don't forget to celebrate! Celebrating student successes—big or small--is important because it sends the message that their hard work is paying off and encourages future success. It also boosts student confidence in their abilities.

There are many ways to celebrate and they don't necessarily need to be extrinsic rewards. Certificates and bulletin boards are great options for celebrations. They are visual and something students can be proud of. If you are going to celebrate with whole class visuals, make the recognition about achieving a goal without calling out levels. Refrain from displaying reading levels or other identifiers that might embarrass the student and take the focus off their achievement. You can celebrate success by giving out awards or prizes such as bookmarks or candy but give extrinsic rewards sparingly. Celebrating student success can also motivate others who may not have achieved their goal yet but are working towards reaching it.

Celebrating success with students is a powerful way to motivate them and build a positive classroom culture. By acknowledging and celebrating student progress and achievement, teachers can create a supportive learning environment where students are inspired to reach their full potential.

## *Final Thoughts*

1. Setting academic goals that are attainable, reasonable and personalized for the individual student is critical for student success.
2. Help students reflect on their progress and evaluate their actions to determine what changes they can make to meet their goal.
3. Students should be involved in the goal-setting process and understand the skills they are working towards.
4. Teachers must create opportunities for students to monitor their own progress using tools like checklists, rubrics, and other appropriate aides.
5. Acknowledging and celebrating progress creates a supportive learning environment.

# 5

# Using Technology to Enhance Learning

*If we teach today as we taught yesterday, we rob our children of tomorrow.* - John Dewey

In today's technologically advanced world, incorporating digital tools in the secondary ELA classroom offers various benefits for students. Technology provides learners with access to a wealth of information that they can leverage to enhance their learning experience. Moreover, it promotes collaboration, which is critical for developing 21st-century skills.

Technology can also be used to create engaging and interactive assignments that challenge students to apply critical thinking skills. Instead of traditional paper/pencil activities, teachers can create or utilize collaborative assignments through Google Documents or Google Slides and various other programs where more than one student can work on a task at the same time. This makes group projects more manageable and efficient.

Peer-to-peer discussions, as explored in chapter 3, play a crucial role in fostering collaboration and enhancing critical thinking skills among students. However, it is important to acknowledge that these discussions can sometimes be limited by the composition of the student group. Online book discussions, on the other hand, offer a unique opportunity to cultivate a sense of community among learners on a broader scale. By enabling interactions among students from different classes, or even different school buildings, throughout the day, these virtual discussions facilitate diverse insights and perspectives on literature. Consequently, they enhance the overall quality and depth of the discourse, enriching the learning experience for all participants involved.

One of the most significant advantages of technology in the classroom is its ability to personalize student learning. With digital tools, students can tailor their learning experience to suit their interests and abilities, thus increasing their motivation and willingness to engage. In particular, reading online is powerful, as it fosters engagement and interest in reading. By leveraging online reading resources and interactive tools, students can explore reading materials collaboratively, analyze and discover new ideas, and become independent readers and thinkers.

By integrating technology into secondary ELA assignments, teachers can empower students with essential 21st-century skills that have practical applications in both college and career settings. These skills encompass creativity, collaboration, critical thinking, and communication, which are highly sought after in today's workforce. Introducing technology in the classroom equips students with the necessary digital literacy skills that are increasingly essential in higher education and professional environments. The utilization of technology has the transformative potential to revolutionize the learning experience, enabling students to actively engage with literature and develop the competencies required for future success.

### *Technology in the ELA Classroom*

Using technology in the classroom can captivate students' attention and deepen their understanding of the texts they read. In the context of English Language Arts, technology can be especially useful in fostering collaborative learning environments and encouraging critical thinking skills. In this section, we will explore a variety of activities that teachers can fuse together to incorporate technology with their reading curriculum. These activities include tools for collaborative reading and personalized book recommendations, offering different ways to enhance students' reading experience, increase motivation, and cultivate a love for literature.

The following activities provide opportunities for students to engage with literature in innovative and meaningful ways:

**Personalized Reading Recommendations:**

Personalized reading recommendations can be a powerful tool for promoting engagement and interest in reading. In addition to using online tools like goodreads, Scholastic Book Wizard, or BookPage, teachers can also encourage students to create recommendation boards for the class. Creating personalized reading recommendation boards is an interactive way for students to share their favorite books with their peers.

Just as we discussed in Chapter 2, students are more likely to take a recommendation from their peers than from their teacher. By sharing their thoughts and opinions about the books they are reading on a class created recommendation board, students can engage in meaningful conversations and discussions about literature. This activity also encourages a sense of community in the class, as they are all working together to create something that is beneficial for everyone.

Personalized reading recommendation boards can be a valuable addition to any classroom reading curriculum. By empowering students to share their opinions and engage in a meaningful dialogue about literature, teachers can create a dynamic and interactive learning environment that promotes a love of reading.

**Collaborative Reading:**

Collaborative reading is a another way to motivate students to engage in the reading process and promote a deeper understanding of texts as collaborative reading requires students to work with their peers. By encouraging students to read and discuss texts together, teachers can foster a collaborative learning environment that encourages critical thinking, communication, and active participation.

One way to incorporate collaborative reading into the classroom is by using digital tools such as Google Docs or Microsoft Teams. These platforms allow students to work together in real-time, share comments, and ask questions about the text they are reading.

By using collaborative reading and an online tool such as Google Docs, you can easily differentiate by assigning groups different articles on the same topic. Here's an example of how it looks in the classroom:

1. Divide students into small groups and assign them an article - everyone can have the same article or you can differentiate by reading levels.
2. Have students use Google Doc to read and annotate the text together as a small group. For example, they can highlight important passages, add comments, or pose questions to each other using the tools already inside Google.
3. Encourage students to use the document to discuss the text as they read. They can ask each other questions, share their interpretations, and make connections to other texts or experiences.
4. After completing the reading assignment, bring the groups back together for a class discussion. Ask each group to share their insights and highlight key points from their collaborative reading discussion.
5. Use a shared document to create a class summary of the text, incorporating ideas from each group.

Use collaborative reading to encourage students to read and discuss texts together, allowing students to share comments, ask questions, and work together on reading assignments. By using technology, you can slow down or speed up the conversation so students are able to work at their own pace. This approach also allows students to learn from each other, build critical thinking skills, and deepen their understanding of the text.

**Online Book Clubs**

One of the benefits of book clubs in secondary ELA is the ability for students to read a common book of their choice and work through that book at their own pace (within the guidelines the teacher sets, of course!). Incorporating technology into book clubs allows teachers to expand book clubs to different classes throughout the day so students of similar abilities or interests can work together.

There are many online platforms - Padlet is a popular online discussion board platform - but teachers can also create their own discussion board using tools such as Google Docs or Google Slides. Many LMS systems such as Canvas also have a discussion board option built in. These platforms provide students with a space to share their thoughts, opinions, and questions about what they are reading in a digital format accessible to everyone in the group.

Here are some ideas on how teachers can use online discussion boards to facilitate book club discussions:

1. Allow students to choose a book they want to read.
2. Create a discussion board on Padlet or Google Docs and share it with each student in the group. You can include prompts or questions to guide the discussion or allow students to start their own threads.
3. Encourage students to participate in the discussion board by sharing their thoughts, opinions, and questions about the book. Remind students to be respectful of their classmates and to engage in meaningful discussions. If you notice students struggling to engage, you can require a specific number of comments by each student.

4. Remember to monitor the discussion board regularly and respond to students' comments and questions - and don't forget to check that all students are making appropriate comments. Use this as an opportunity to further the discussion or clarify any misunderstandings.
5. After the discussions are complete, review the board as a class and highlight key points or themes that emerged. You can also review the discussion board for each book as a small group discussion.

Online book clubs offer students the opportunity to participate in book discussions in a digital space, accessible anytime and anywhere. This flexibility allows for varied groupings and a wider selection of book choices for teachers to offer. Moreover, these online discussions foster critical thinking skills as students engage with the text and express their thoughts and opinions in a respectful and productive manner. By utilizing online book clubs, teachers can encourage meaningful dialogue, enhance students' comprehension of the literature, and cultivate a sense of community within the classroom.

## *Incorporate Digital Reading into Your Classroom*

As technology continues to shape every aspect of modern life, it is increasingly essential to explore its potential to enhance learning in the classroom. In particular, digital tools and resources can offer numerous benefits to secondary ELA students by providing them with access to information, facilitating collaboration and communication, and personalizing their learning experience. In this section, we will explore how teachers can integrate technology into the secondary ELA classroom to create a more engaging and equitable learning environment for students.

Here are some ideas on how you can bring digital reading into your classroom:

- Provide access to e-books through an online library, either through your district or your local public library.
- Allow students to listen to audiobooks which can increase comprehension and improve reading skills when paired with the written text.
- Encourage students to use e-books for research projects or assignments related to specific topics instead of being dependent on random google searches.

### *Audiobooks and Ebooks*

Introducing audiobooks and ebooks into the secondary English Language Arts (ELA) classroom can greatly enhance the reading experience for students. By incorporating these digital resources, teachers can create an engaging and flexible learning environment that promotes a love for reading and caters to individual student needs.

Digital reading materials offer a wide variety of benefits and opportunities for students. They provide access to a vast range of texts, allowing students to explore diverse genres, authors, and topics that may not be readily available in traditional print books. This exposure to a wide array of materials can broaden students' perspectives and foster a deeper appreciation for literature.

Audiobooks and ebooks offer accessibility and flexibility that traditional print books don't. Students can access digital resources from their own devices, at any time and place, allowing for seamless integration into their daily lives. This accessibility eliminates barriers such as limited library hours.

As educators, it is important to embrace digital resources and integrate them into your ELA curriculum. By doing so, teachers can nurture a lifelong love for reading, equip students with essential literacy skills, and foster an inclusive learning environment that meets the diverse needs of all students.

In the following sections, we will explore some of the most important reasons for using audiobooks and ebooks in the classroom, as well as provide tips and resources for getting started.

## Audio Books

Audiobooks offer a range of benefits that traditional print books cannot match. For example, audiobooks provide an immersive listening experience that can help students develop their listening and comprehension skills, while also offering an opportunity to explore books they may not have been able to read on their own. When an audiobook is combined with the student following along with the written text, it helps improve student reading abilities.

Audiobooks keep students who are reading below grade level interested in reading. Too many times students reading below grade level are subjected to stories that are also below their maturity level. It's important to recognize that secondary students who feel a book is too simplistic or juvenile are less likely to engage with it.

Reluctant readers often view audiobooks as a form of "cheating" or "getting away with something" because they are not engaging in the traditional act of reading. However, this perception can actually work in favor of these students. By introducing audiobooks as an alternative reading option, teachers can entice reluctant readers to give books a chance. Once students become engrossed in the story and realize the enjoyment and benefits they can derive from it, they may be more inclined to explore other forms of reading, such as print books.

Audiobooks also provide reluctant readers with a sense of independence. By listening to a book, they have control over their reading experience. This freedom empowers students to take ownership of their learning and encourages them to explore books they may not have considered before.

Overall, audiobooks have proven to be a valuable resource in promoting reading and engaging students. By providing an alternative to traditional print books, audiobooks can ignite a passion for stories, enhance comprehension skills, and nurture a love for reading among students who may have fallen behind or are considered reluctant readers.

**E-Books**

Ebooks offer a wide range of advantages that cater to the needs and preferences of today's digital learners. One of the key benefits of ebooks is their accessibility from any online device. Students can access their reading material anywhere at anytime, without being restricted by library hours or concerns about overdue books. This flexibility is particularly beneficial for students with time constraints due to family circumstances or busy schedules.

Another advantage of ebooks is their ability to meet students where they are in today's digital age. With the increasing prevalence of digital devices, students are used to consuming information in a digital format. Ebooks provide a familiar and comfortable reading experience by displaying content in an easy-to-read format on their device. This accessibility reduces barriers and intimidation that some students may feel when faced with traditional print books.

Additionally, ebooks offer a level of flexibility and customization that can be tailored to individual students' needs. Students can adjust font size, line spacing, and other settings to create a personalized reading experience that suits their specific needs. This customization promotes engagement and motivation, leading to improved reading comprehension and enjoyment.

Many ebooks offer a range of interactive features that can engage and motivate students during their reading experience. These features include things such as multimedia elements, interactive quizzes, and the ability to highlight and annotate text, empowering students to interact with the content and enhance their comprehension. By embracing ebooks, teachers create an inclusive and flexible reading environment that accommodates diverse schedules and learning preferences, while fostering continuous engagement and enthusiasm for reading.

By embracing ebooks, teachers create an inclusive and adaptable reading environment that accommodates the diverse learning styles and needs of their students. The accessibility, interactive features, and personalized experience offered by ebooks support continuous engagement, foster a love for reading, and enable students to thrive in the digital era.

## *Online Libraries*

Online libraries provide several advantages for secondary students that are not available through traditional brick and mortar libraries. One major benefit is the convenience and accessibility they offer. With online libraries, students can access books instantly on any device available, including laptops, phones, or tablets making it a more equitable option.

Online libraries provide students with 24/7 access to reading material, so even when physical libraries are closed or a physical copy of a book is not available, students can still access books. Online libraries take away the need for students to find transportation to the library if they are not old enough to drive because they simply need to access their device to access the books. This allows students to read anywhere, anytime which promotes greater ownership of the time they devote to reading outside of class and encourages students to read more frequently.

Online libraries offer a wider range of resources than traditional libraries because they are not limited by physical space. With an online library, students can search for books from different authors and genres, find educational videos to aid in their learning, access primary sources for research projects, and even listen to audio recordings of some texts. Online libraries make it easy for students to explore different topics.

Another advantage of online libraries is they offer customization options that can improve the reading experience for students. In addition to being able to adjust the font size, font style, and background color, many online libraries have the ability to make recommendations based on what a student has previously read, keeping them engaged even when they have finished a book. Students can also access translation options to read books in their native language or a foreign language they are studying.

Online libraries offer secondary students a multitude of benefits, including equity, convenience, accessibility, and customization, making them an invaluable resource. By providing students with a platform that goes beyond the physical building, online libraries ensure equal access to a vast range of reading materials, regardless of a student's geographical location or socioeconomic background.

If a school district does not have the option of an online library, teachers need to reach out to the public library in their area. Typically, all that is needed to gain access to the online catalog is a current library card. Most public libraries will work with teachers to help ensure each student is able to obtain a library card.

Ultimately, online libraries empower secondary students with the freedom to explore, discover, and embrace the joy of reading, contributing to their overall educational and personal growth.

## Preparing Students for 21st-Century

In the 21st century, the ability to read remains a crucial skill students must acquire. With the ever-expanding availability of information through various media formats, such as books, websites, and social media, students with strong reading skills have a significant advantage. Therefore, teachers need to prioritize teaching reading and its associated skills in today's educational landscape.

Unfortunately, teaching students to read is not enough. Teachers must also focus on developing critical thinking and digital literacy skills to help students navigate and comprehend the large amount of information they encounter. An essential aspect for teachers to address is teaching students how to critically evaluate sources. Given the abundance of online information, it is crucial for students to discern reliable from unreliable sources. Students must learn to consider factors like authority, bias, and accuracy when assessing information. Additionally, students need to acquire fact-checking and verification skills.

The good news is that digital literacy doesn't have to fall all the ELA teacher. All teachers should incorporate technology into their lessons and provide opportunities for students to practice using digital tools effectively. By doing so, students can enhance their critical thinking and digital literacy skills, enabling them to become more discerning consumers of information.

Reading skills have a profound impact on a student's future success. Reading proficiency is essential for academic achievement across all subjects, including science, history, and literature. Proficient readers can comprehend and analyze complex ideas more effectively, leading to higher academic performance.

Furthermore, strong reading skills are crucial in the professional world. As technology continues to reshape the nature of work, the ability to read and comprehend information quickly and accurately has become an indispensable skill. Industries such as healthcare, finance, and technology all require workers to possess strong reading skills to understand intricate information.

Secondary ELA teachers must continue to prioritize teaching students to read in the 21st century. By emphasizing critical thinking and digital literacy skills, teachers can empower students as they navigate the vast sea of information available to them. As society continually adapts to the fast-paced changes of this century, the ability to read will only grow in importance for success in all areas of life.

## *Final Thoughts*

1. Incorporating technology into the secondary ELA classroom offers several benefits, including personalization of student learning.
2. Technology promotes a love of literature by using online resources and interactive tools that allow students to explore reading materials collaboratively, analyze and discover new ideas, and become independent readers.
3. Technology fosters a sense of community among learners, as they share their insights and perspectives on literature with their peers through online book discussions or collaborative reading.

4. By embracing ebooks and audiobooks, teachers create an inclusive and adaptable reading experience that accommodates the diverse needs of their students.
5. Strong reading skills remain an important 21st-century skill, with the ability to evaluate sources critically and digital literacy being essential.
6. A strong ability to read can lead to academic and career success in various fields.

# 6

# Navigating the New Educational Landscape

*The people who are crazy enough to think they can change the world are he one who do it. - Steve Jobs*

As teachers continue to navigate these first few years post pandemic, they will continue to face challenges. Teachers will continue to be confronted by learning gaps - missed pieces of learning in a student's education. Teachers will continue to be confronted by challenges they've never faced, nor have they been trained for. It can be incredibly frustrating and defeating for teachers to feel like they are working harder than ever, yet it never seems to be enough. As a nation, we must recognize the need to support educators and continue to work towards giving teachers the support and resources they need to overcome the challenges brought on by the pandemic.

Life is not back to normal no matter how many times district personnel and politicians want to say it is. Simply saying it doesn't magically fill in the gaps and missed opportunities students faced. Two years of in person learning is not going to bring students back to pre-pandemic levels, especially when the expectation is that students learn missed concepts in addition to meeting current grade level standards. Not to mention how many students are not yet ready to face school and need mental health support to learn how to deal with the trauma they have faced.

The ideas offered in this book are meant to provide educators with options - a recognition that you are teaching material that was previously two or three grade levels below your current grade. Teachers who are currently teaching middle school are having to teach concepts students previously learned in upper elementary in order to fill in gaps. This is not putting the blame on elementary teachers, it is simply recognizing that during the pandemic school was different, the material was presented differently, the support given to students was different and students participated in school differently. Now that teachers and students are back in the classroom, every teacher regardless of the grade level they teach, must find ways to identify and fill in the learning gaps.

The challenges that teachers are facing in the aftermath of the pandemic are significant and cannot be ignored. The learning gaps that students have experienced will require educators to modify their teaching methods and provide more individualized options for students. It is crucial that teachers receive the support and resources they need to overcome these challenges and help their students succeed. As a nation, we must recognize the importance of investing in education and prioritize the well-being of teachers, staff and students. With dedication and perseverance, we can work together to overcome the obstacles presented by the pandemic and create a brighter future for our students.

## *Teachers and Students Must Work Together*

Teachers and students both play important roles in creating a better educational experience. The pandemic has presented unique challenges, but by working together, educators and students can overcome these obstacles. While it is not necessary to throw away everything teachers know about teaching, it is important that they understand how to modify their approach to meet the needs of their students. A one size fits all approach to education has never worked, as most teachers can attest, and the need to individualize and differentiate lessons is stronger now than ever before.

Recognizing the challenges posed by the pandemic is the first step towards establishing a learning environment that addresses the gaps. By acknowledging the difficulties that students encounter, teachers can adapt their teaching strategies to meet the individual needs of students. This approach fosters greater student engagement and motivation, ultimately leading to improved academic performance.

Another effective method of collaboration between teachers and students is to create a culture of reading. Encouraging reading for the sake of reading can significantly enhance student literacy, vocabulary, and critical thinking skills. It cultivates empathy and a deeper understanding of diverse people and cultures. Teachers can collaborate with students to select books that capture their interest, curate reading lists, and facilitate discussions centered around the literature. By offering students choices, educators assist in nurturing a lifelong love for learning and an appreciation for the power of literature.

Setting personalized academic goals is another way that teachers and students can work together to create a better educational experience. Teaching students how to set and monitor goals helps to shift the responsibility of learning from teacher to student. By setting individual goals, students take ownership of their learning and focus on areas where they need improvement. Teachers must provide guidance and support, helping students identify their strengths and weaknesses and develop strategies for achieving their goals. As students learn to monitor their own progress they can see how they are progressing. This gives students a say in what is happening with their own education.

Incorporating technology into the learning process is also a key component of a collaborative learning environment. Technology provides students with access to a wealth of educational resources, and facilitates communication between teachers, students, and families. It allows for more personalized learning experiences. Teachers can use online tools, such as Google Apps and learning management systems, to create interactive lessons and track student progress. Students can also use technology to collaborate with each other, share ideas, and engage in online discussions.

Developing a shared vision and common goals fosters a more efficient collaboration between teachers and students. When there is a collective objective, a sense of ownership and commitment towards the learning process is cultivated by both sides. Teachers can actively engage students in the goal-setting process, encouraging them to identify their strengths and determine the specific steps and strategies for achieving those goals. Through the creation of a shared vision, teachers and students establish a welcoming learning environment that promotes a sense of unity and purpose.

## *Encouraging Educators for Tomorrow*

For teachers who may feel overwhelmed or discouraged by the new educational landscape, it is important to remember that learning and adapting to changes is an ongoing process. A process that occurred prior to the pandemic and is simply part of the profession. Teachers are constantly striving to improve their craft and provide the best possible learning experiences for their students. The pandemic, however, brought unique challenges to the forefront, but let's not ignore the fact the pandemic has also created opportunities for growth and innovation in education.

One way to stay motivated and engaged in teaching is to seek out professional development opportunities. Many organizations and institutions offer virtual training and resources that can help teachers stay current on best practices and innovative teaching strategies. Additionally, networking with other educators can provide valuable insights and support for navigating the challenges of the new educational landscape. Teachers across the country are collaborating to host online conferences in order to share lessons and stories from today's classroom and provide encouragement to colleagues.

It is important for teachers to remember that they are not alone in navigating this new normal. By supporting and encouraging each other, teachers can overcome the challenges and continue to provide quality education to their students. It is essential for teachers to establish strong connections and support networks within the teaching community. Collaborating and sharing ideas with colleagues not only foster professional growth, but also provides emotional support during challenging times. Engaging in professional development opportunities, attending conferences, and participating in online forums can expand a teacher's network and provide access to valuable support.

Teachers are encouraged to remain focused on providing personalized instruction and support to help students succeed - even if this is not the popular choice in their school. Teachers are the professionals and they know what is best for the students sitting in their classroom.

Teachers also need to keep an open mind and be willing to try new things. As you explore new teaching strategies and technologies, share your successes and challenges with others. By supporting each other, teachers can learn and grow together.

Stay positive and resilient as you can as you navigate this new educational landscape. To do this, teachers need to prioritize their own well-being and build a strong support system. A challenging profession like teaching becomes even more demanding during times of uncertainty, such as the pandemic. By staying flexible, focusing on controllable aspects in the classroom, and leaning on colleagues, teachers can provide quality education while supporting each other.

And, don't forget celebrating small victories and acknowledging achievements, both big and small, can greatly contribute to maintaining a positive outlook. Recognizing student progress, creative teaching strategies, and personal accomplishments can boost morale and motivation for both teachers and students.

By implementing these strategies and nurturing a positive mindset, teachers can navigate the evolving educational landscape with resilience, adaptability, and a commitment to providing quality education for their students.

# Meet the Author

After returning to the classroom after two years of remote teaching, Carolyn noticed a significant difference in her student's skill levels and realized that she needed to adapt her teaching methods to meet the needs of all learners.

In order to create a student-centered learning environment where all students could feel safe and successful, Carolyn started to search for effective strategies that would engage, motivate, and build relationships with her students, while also providing them with the appropriate instruction to fill in the gaps left by remote learning.

Drawing on her own experiences as a teacher still in the classroom, Carolyn wrote a book to inspire and support other educators during these unprecedented times. She hopes to encourage teachers that they are not alone on their journey. Motivating Readers: Teaching in the Post Pandemic Era provides teachers with ideas, techniques, and insights to navigate the ever-changing educational system and help their students succeed. While it may take some time to recover from the pandemic, all hope is not lost.

For more information and resources to implement the ideas presented in the book, please go to **www.middleschoolcafe.com.**

You can find the author on social media at **Instagram** (@middleschoolcafe), **Secondary ELA Facebook group** (https://www.facebook.com/groups/secondaryela), and **Pinterest** (midschoolcafe).

Carolyn Wahl has a weekly podcast, **Middle School Café Podcast**, where she discusses strategies to help teachers reclaim the ELA Classroom. You can find the podcast in your favorite podcast app.

www.ingramcontent.com/pod-product-compliance
Ingram Content Group UK Ltd.
Pitfield, Milton Keynes, MK11 3LW, UK
UKHW021307180426
11947UKWH00015B/1080